Edward C. Sellner, Ph.D.

Step 5

Telling My Story

Revised Edition

Hazelden
Publishing

Hazelden Publishing
Center City, Minnesota 55012-0176
hazelden.org/bookstore

© 1981, 1992 by Hazelden Foundation.
All rights reserved. Published 1981 (for-
merly titled *The Fifth Step: A Guide to
Reconciliation*). Revised edition 1992
Printed in the United States of America.
No portion of this publication may be
reproduced in any manner without the
written permission of the publisher.

The Twelve Steps are reprinted with permission of
Alcoholics Anonymous World Services, Inc. Permission to reprint the Twelve Steps does not mean that
Alcoholics Anonymous has reviewed or approved the
contents of this publication, nor that AA agrees with
the views expressed herein. The views expressed
herein are solely those of the author. AA is a program
of recovery from alcoholism. Use of the Twelve Steps
in connection with programs and activities that are
patterned after AA, but that address other problems,
does not imply otherwise.

*Admitted to God, to ourselves, and to
another human being the exact nature of
our wrongs.*

—STEP FIVE

A personal experience

There was a time in my life when I lived without hope. Given much, I was grateful for little; surrounded by a culture, religion, and heritage of beliefs, I affirmed nothing as my own; living in what I thought was freedom, I felt only chaos and confusion within. In the darkness of a cave, one can hear only echoes of emptiness.

At last, when I could no longer stand this sense of hopelessness, I reached out to a person, a friend who was there when I needed someone or something—I didn't know what. This person listened to my story, said yes when I had been hearing only no, and accepted without judgment my fears, despair, loneliness, selfishness, and inner darkness. A flame flickered in the night, and it seemed that suddenly there was a God, a Higher Power greater than any one of us, who moves like a consuming fire or a gentle breeze or a rushing wave in the lives of individuals and nations.

My experience with this person who listened to my Fifth Step was a transforming experience, one that revealed to me a God who had always been so close and yet so far away. It was a turning point. It was the beginning of a way out of the darkness of the cave, and though many stumblings and falls have occurred since then, the vague outline of the cave's entrance was perceived at last.

Acceptance comes from telling our story

What I learned from that experience is this: we cannot change anything unless we acknowledge and accept it first. Self-knowledge and self-acceptance depend upon telling our story, being heard by someone other than ourselves—and, perhaps most importantly, hearing ourselves speak.

This is the opinion of many different spiritual traditions. Teachers of the ancient Greeks advised those seeking inner healing, "Give up what you have, and you will receive." Shamans, the spiritual leaders of Native Americans and other tribal cultures, warned their people that difficulties not shared could make a person sick. Early desert hermits told those who came to them for guidance that everything in one's heart needs to be confessed to an elder, a wise and holy person, for "an evil thought sheds its danger only when it is brought into the light."

These traditions and others like them affirm that it is only when we verbally acknowledge our feelings, past faults, and destructive patterns of behavior to another human being that they lose their power over us. Then we are given real freedom to move on.

We need Step Five to stay sober

The co-founders of AA, Bill Wilson and Dr. Bob Smith, held some of the same beliefs when they included Step Five in their Twelve Steps: "Admitted to God, to ourselves, and to another human being the exact nature of our wrongs." From their own experiences and work with recovering alcoholics, they believed that the Fifth Step was one of the most necessary of all the Steps. Without it, they said, the alcoholic might never overcome the compulsion to drink (or abuse other drugs). According to them, whether one confesses to a clergyperson, doctor, psychologist, family member, or friend, telling all of one's story—all those things that stand in the way of forgiveness and reconciliation—is considered vital to long-term sobriety and peace of mind.

Getting past excuses

Bill W. and Dr. Bob also admitted that Step Five was one of the most difficult Steps to take and one of the most often avoided. Why is that? Each of us can find a "good" reason—or an excuse. Some of us say, "I don't have to tell anyone about my past; I'm already forgiven by God." Some say, quite honestly, "I wouldn't know where to begin." Others tell themselves, "It's nobody's business, anyway." Many of us put it off, saying, "I'm not ready"—one of the best excuses to justify our procrastination for a long, long time. . . .

The fact is that most of us find it extremely difficult to be honest with ourselves, let alone someone else. Deep down we're afraid of what might happen if we did open up. We risk the possibility that our listener might not like us after all, or, perhaps worse, that we might dislike ourselves even more. For many of us the pain of going into the past seems too overwhelming, considering the guilt, regret, and shame we may have tried so hard to bury.

Still, as the "Big Book" (*Alcoholics Anonymous*) says, unless we are entirely honest with someone else, we cannot "expect to live long or happily in this world."* The Fifth Step is our chance to do so.

Alcoholics Anonymous [the Big Book], 3d ed. (New York: AA World Services, Inc., 1976), 74. All subsequent references to the Big Book are from this edition.

3

How this pamphlet can help you

This pamphlet is written for those who want to pull themselves out of their fears, despondency, despair, or procrastination; for those who want greater self-acceptance, healing of the past, and hope for a better future. It is written from the perspective of what has worked for me, and what others have told me works for them. As a guide, it does not have all the answers. Only you, the reader, with the help of your friends and your Higher Power, can find those for yourself. Nevertheless, the following guidelines can give you some direction:

- Start with Step Four.
- Choose a friendly listener.
- Tell your story.
- Let go and let God.
- Make the Fifth Step an ongoing event.

Start with Step Four

Anyone who is considering a Fifth Step needs to begin with the Fourth. There is a definite progression in the Twelve Steps, and they are meant to be taken in order. All twelve are part of a total process leading to what the Big Book calls a "spiritual awakening." This is a personality change or transformation, a new state of consciousness and being—the discovery that life does have meaning and that we too can experience spiritual progress one day at a time.

Step Four is concerned with a "searching and fearless moral inventory." It asks us to take stock of our lives, an ancient practice that the Irish, among other cultures, associate with "soul-making"; that is, reviewing the direction of our lives and attempting to

4

make peace with the physical and spiritual worlds—
so closely interconnected—and find our place within
them.

What Step Four requires
The Big Book speaks of this discipline as getting at
the "truth" of who we are. Since memory can be the
greatest teacher, this Step of self-evaluation asks us to
look at where we have come from and what patterns
of living have been ours. Such a task is not easy for
anyone. It requires such basics as time, a quiet environment, and writing materials. It also requires certain qualities in us that no one else can provide.
  Let's look at these basics in more detail:

- First, getting at the truth of our lives and re-
  collecting our pasts (finding the pieces) take
  time. At the outset, we may need to *make time* if
  we are really going to bring to light past memories and discover what they have to teach us. We
  can begin with a daily or weekly schedule for
  ourselves and set aside a certain time each day
  or every few days to do Step Four. It's also use-
  ful to set a deadline for completing the Fourth
  Step so that it doesn't go on indefinitely.
- Second, we need to find a *quiet place* in our
  home or, if we are in a treatment center, some
  part of the unit where there is space for reflection. If it is possible, going to a retreat center or
  a cabin at a lake, seashore, mountain, or desert
  can also provide the type of environment that
  contributes to our soul-searching.
- Third, we need to find *something to write on* or
  record our memories in, such as a notebook or a

journal (preferably one with a hard cover that will protect the pages from getting scattered or lost).

The advantages of writing
Although speaking into a tape recorder can be a way of activating our memories, writing something down with a pencil or pen is especially helpful. This process of re-membering the past (putting it back together) often happens only when we begin to write. Self-destructive patterns, as well as those patterns that contribute to our happiness, are often perceived only in retrospect. In writing we discover aspects of our personalities and areas of our lives previously overlooked.

However we go about it, the writing usually clarifies what sort of person we have become, for good and for ill. It also reveals what aspects of ourselves we need to acknowledge, accept, and change if we are to experience forgiveness and healing.

It's not necessary that everything be clear in our minds before we begin, that we have perfect essays composed ahead of time. In fact, perfectionism is one characteristic that most of us need to avoid! The important thing is to get something on paper. All of the Twelve Steps are about *taking action*, not just sitting and trying to think things through. Thus once we have set aside some time and found a quiet place, we just need to sit down and start.

Looking at periods in our lives
When we take a Fourth Step for the first time, we go back to our earliest memories. Then we divide our lives into ten-year periods, sketching out roughly

where we were and what was going on. If we have already taken one or more Fourth Steps, we go back to the last worthwhile one we made.

If you are new to this process or want more help, read the Big Book (pages 58-88) and *Twelve Steps and Twelve Traditions* (pages 42-62).* Both can help clarify the Fourth and Fifth Steps. A Fourth Step guidebook can also help.

Searching for character defects
Once we have a rough idea of where we want to go with our Fourth Step, we can begin to fill in the years. We look for certain things that have contributed to our unhappiness, dependencies, and addictive behaviors.

The Big Book suggests that in Step Four we take "inventory" of all the anger and resentments, the deceptions and lies, the pain and guilt and grief that may have accumulated over the years. This honest evaluation includes a search for personality flaws, or what AA calls "character defects." Among them are dishonesty, selfishness, pride, intolerance, impatience, envy, phoniness, self-pity, and letting ourselves be dominated by fear. Together with chemical dependency, these defects may be the cause of disrupted lives and ruined relationships.

The first things to focus on in this inventory are resentments: those indignations and slights that can quite literally destroy us. From them, the Big Book says, come "all forms of spiritual disease."** Those of us taking the Fourth Step for the first time will want to go as far back as we can in early childhood

---

**Twelve Steps and Twelve Traditions* (New York: AA World Services, Inc., 1981).

** *Alcoholics Anonymous*, 64.

and make a list of those people, often our parents or parental figures, whom we may still resent.

Besides bringing resentments out in the open, any Fourth Step should unearth areas that are now causing or have caused a great deal of grief, hurt, anger, frustration, or guilt. It should bring to light all those unresolved feelings, unhealed memories, and personal defects that have produced depression and loss of self-worth. We need to acknowledge any secrets which, though "safely" hidden, still continue to divide us within. According to the Swiss psychologist Carl Jung, those things we seek to avoid talking about are a kind of "psychic poison," dividing us from others and our better selves.

Being honest and thorough
Honesty is of primary importance in this search. Without it, the Fifth Step will not only be worthless, it will also be yet another self-deception we may have already experienced too many times before.

Thoroughness also helps. Anything worthwhile takes time, care, and patience—qualities we often find in short supply. If the Fifth Step is to be well done, the Fourth cannot be rushed. We cannot expect to complete it in a day. To go back over a lifetime—especially if it is our first Fourth Step—and discover what went wrong takes time and care.

If we are to be thorough, we need to write *specific* examples of behavior and feelings related to *specific* episodes and memories—not vague generalities that could apply to anyone. We need to name concretely what happened, when and where it happened, and with or to whom. Only then might an overall destructive pattern or character defect be revealed.

Though thoroughness in Step Four is necessary, it should not be equated with scrupulousness. This is another form of perfectionism; we mistakenly think that *every* little detail in our lives must be acknowledged. While Fourth Step guidebooks can be of help in this regard, the advice and experience of a sponsor or friend who has already done a Fourth Step can be a major resource.

Finding balance
Besides requiring honesty and thoroughness, a good Fourth Step needs balance. This means focusing not only on our liabilities and defects but also on our assets: the God-given strengths, talents, and gifts that we all possess. We try to find and acknowledge those gifts that we can give to others, and those things for which we're grateful. Searching for them may be the most difficult task in preparing the Fourth Step, since many of us are burdened with guilt, remorse, and a low sense of self-worth. Again, it is here that a friend or AA group can do the most to help us discover our positive attributes and begin to gain a more balanced, realistic perspective.

Often, however, those of us suffering from a poor self-image or feelings of low self-esteem will truly feel greater self-acceptance only *after* completing Step Five. Before that, claiming any assets may be more of an intellectual exercise than a conviction of both mind and heart. The important thing is that we try to name our assets and listen closely to those who know us.

Experiencing the rewards
Writing an honest, thorough, and balanced Step Four is a rewarding experience. (Most of us acquire

these qualities only by actually doing the Steps rather than waiting for assurance that we possess them!)

Although perhaps painful at times, taking the Fourth Step can lead to increased self-knowledge and even a great sense of relief. One woman described her Step Four experience to me as a "revolutionary way" of self-discovery. She began to have a more realistic and compassionate view of herself and her past without the self-delusions that blind all of us at times.

Choose a friendly listener

While preparing for a Fourth Step, begin thinking of people who could hear your Fifth Step. The Big Book says that almost anyone will do: a clergyperson, doctor, or counselor; a family member who will not be adversely affected by our total honesty; a sponsor, friend, or even a stranger.

Qualities to look for

There are, however, certain qualities in a listener that can make your Fifth Step a more positive experience:

- First, the person should have the *ability to keep things in confidence.* He or she should appreciate the highly confidential nature of what you reveal in the Fifth Step and not share the contents with anyone. In other words, the Fifth Step listener should be what the Big Book calls "close-mouthed."

- Second, such a person should have an *understanding of the Fifth Step itself.* He or she should know the significance of the Step and the need for any chemically dependent person to take it. In other words, the listener should not only be familiar with the Twelve Steps but should also be attempting to live them.

- Third, the person should demonstrate *maturity and wisdom* based on his or her personal experience of constructively dealing with chemical dependency or other serious problems. To be of any help to you when you take your Fifth Step, the listener should have some understanding of and compassion toward self and others. This includes a broad view of human nature and the ability to see destructive and constructive patterns of behavior in others' lives because a person is familiar with them in his or her own life.
- Fourth, the potential listener should be *willing to share personal examples* from his or her life. This sharing elicits greater confidence and self-disclosure. Every good Fifth Step is to some degree a dialogue, not a monologue. If the listener is unwilling to enter into a two-way relationship, the experience of reconciliation will suffer.

The kind of person that we need for a good Fifth Step, then, is someone who can be trusted; someone who is respected yet compassionate; someone who inspires more comfort than fear; someone who is to some degree a friend. A listener does not have to be a close friend, but he or she should at least be a receptive listener and a discerning guide.

Taking the initiative
Granted, a Fifth Step listener with these attributes is not always readily available. If we want to have a good Fifth Step, however, our task is to look and ask around. Some of us may go to a clergyperson because

11

we believe confidentiality will be guaranteed. If so, we should try to find someone from our own religious denomination; this may allow for greater rapport. Whoever we choose should be someone who understands and appreciates AA's program and the role of the Fifth Step.

If we are in a treatment center, we do not always get to choose our Fifth Step listener. In that case, we should take some initiative and get acquainted with the minister or listener before our Fifth Step. That effort can make the difference between a positive, open Fifth Step and one characterized by anxiety, defensiveness, and inability to reveal all that needs to be said.

Familiarity does not have to breed contempt; it can, in fact, foster openness and trust. After all, it is the unknown we fear. And though AA literature states that a stranger may suffice, strangers are not always trustworthy. They might easily misunderstand us or be easily misunderstood and thus will not help our experience of reconciliation.

Taking all of this into account, we need to go ahead and ask our potential listener, explore what we hope to accomplish, and allow that person to explain his or her own expectations. We also need to ask any questions we have. Together we then set up a time to meet for Step Five, understanding that most Fifth Steps, if they are to be truly beneficial, usually take not less than an hour and no longer than three.

Tell your story

When we have completed the Fourth Step inventory and chosen a friendly listener, it is time to begin the Fifth Step itself.

Step Four was primarily an attempt to discover the obstacles to a happy and worthwhile life. Step Five is the opportunity, as the Big Book says, for "casting out" those obstacles. If our past is filled with regret and pain, now is the time to change all that and make room for a better future.

How to begin
How do we begin? Quite simply, we sit down across from our Fifth Step listener, pray together for guidance (if we care to do so), and acknowledge any feelings of fear or doubt on our part. Then we start to tell our story, the story of our life—a story that is often neither claimed nor accepted as our own, and thus never fully appreciated.

Alcoholics Anonymous began in 1935 with such an event, when Bill W. and Dr. Bob openly and honestly acknowledged their struggles with alcoholism and their attempts to stay sober. Storytelling today is an essential dynamic of AA. It is also in terms of storytelling that the Fifth Step itself is described in the Big Book: a person is to tell all of his or her story to another human being, all those things that stand in the way of inner and outer reconciliation with self, others, and a Higher Power.

Putting insights in context
Thus when we start Step Five, we should put the insights that emerged from Step Four into the context of our life story. In the Fifth Step we acknowledge all those areas that arose in the "searching and fearless moral inventory" of Step Four, including the

following, which the Big Book and *Twelve Steps and Twelve Traditions* point out:

- Memories: "Every dark cranny of the past," all those "tormenting ghosts of yesterday."
- Character defects: Every "twist of character," obstacle, weakness, and defect that has come to light.
- Feelings of guilt: "The open and honest sharing" of "its terrible burden."
- All those things that "really bother" a person, such as anger, resentments, and unexpressed grief.

Although the wording of Step Five implies that we admit to specific "wrongs," it is clear that we need to share much more. Rather than attempt to cover all of those areas listed above one at a time, we can handle them better by referring to them in the broader context of our lives, beginning with our experiences and memories of childhood.

Somehow, by talking about our early years and proceeding from there, we'll often find the Fifth Step easier to get through. Starting at the beginning of our lives can also help the listener understand more clearly what is being said and see the overall direction of our life journey and emerging character.

Letting the whole story flow
The most important thing for each of us taking Step Five is to *tell all that needs to be told*. If there is anything from the Fourth Step that we would prefer not to share, that is precisely what we need to acknowledge. We can do this either at the very beginning of Step Five or as our life story unfolds.

Whatever has been written down in the Fourth Step is meant to clarify one's life before the Fifth Step itself. Although our written notes or journal can remind us of what to cover, they should not serve as our exact script. In other words, it's important not to adhere strictly to what we have written by reading it aloud one line at a time. Let the story flow. In that context, the listener will find it easier to share aspects of his or her own story. Then we enter into a mutual conversation that can bring about healing effects.

Remembering our purpose
We should keep in mind that we are not doing our Fifth Step to please the listener, *but to heal ourselves.* In self-disclosure we are being totally honest, perhaps for the first time. It is the inner self, the self that is trying to emerge in sobriety and maturity, that we must satisfy.

As we share past deeds or specific incidents, we need not be afraid of shocking, surprising, or scandalizing the listener. This person has probably heard such stories before or experienced them personally. (The psychologist Carl Rogers writes that what is often considered most personal is also most universal.) We should never think that we are the original "great sinner." This is an inverted form of pride that reality and the daily headlines consistently prove to be false.

Experiencing the rewards
Many people who spoke to me about their Fifth Step described it in terms of healing and being cleansed. One person said, "It was as if a ton of bricks had been taken off my shoulders." Another, whose words

15

I will never forget, said, "It was like being saved, like being snatched out of the jaws of death." Whatever the images or terminology, many, like me, have finally come to accept our lives more gratefully as a result of the stories we share in Step Five. We discover a God who is forgiving, available, and worthy of trust. This is a Higher Power found not so much in the distant past and in the stories of other people as in our own suffering—and most mysteriously of all, in the midst of our own sense of failure.

The Big Book and *Twelve Steps and Twelve Traditions* say that many things can happen when we tell our story: an end to the compulsion to drink (or abuse drugs); increased self-knowledge; new self-confidence; relief and release from feelings of guilt; delight; humility; loss of fear; emergence from a terrible sense of isolation; healing tranquility; a sense of gratitude; the ability to begin to forgive others and oneself. Some people, according to the Big Book, may even have a spiritual experience: "Many an A.A., once agnostic or atheist, tells us that it was during this stage of Step Five that he first actually felt the presence of God."

Let go and let God

Considering these potential results, we can see that telling all of our story with the help of another person can be a significant event of reconciliation.

The thing to remember, however, is that no Fifth Step is exactly alike. Not everyone has a dramatic or cathartic experience. I have talked with those who left their Step Five greatly disappointed because they did not. Yet the most important aspect of the Fifth Step is not that we see "results," but that we be honest and do the best we can. As much as the Fifth Step is related to storytelling, it is also related to surrender: the act of "letting go and letting God."

That simple slogan of AA is part of all the Twelve Steps and is the very foundation of recovery. It especially applies as we take the Fifth Step. We must surrender to the process of the Fifth Step by letting go of any compulsive need to control its outcome. We must also let go of any expectations we might have of it—even the desire that it transform our lives. It seems that God (or our Higher Power) works best— as we do—in freedom rather than coercion.

Whatever happens, when we complete our Fifth Step we should tell our listener that we are done and then wait quietly for a response. We let go of our past and turn the results over to our Higher Power. Sometimes it is only then that we discover a compassionate God who understands and forgives. AA says that spiritual awakenings are as diverse as those who experience them. I would add that they frequently happen when we least expect them. We need to accept serenely that Fifth Step experiences will vary as well. If ours is not all that we wanted or hoped for, there will be time for other inventories and other Fifth Steps.

Make the Fifth Step an ongoing event

The practice of making a personal inventory in Step Four and of "housecleaning" in Step Five is not meant to be a once-in-a-lifetime event. Those initial Steps, AA believes, are supposed to become a regular habit. Step Ten, for example, specifically recommends that we continue to take personal inventories and "promptly admit" our wrongs. These annual or semiannual housecleanings contribute to ongoing recovery and help guarantee that sobriety, health, and a greater degree of wholeness will continue.

Two things in particular can help us: having a sponsor or spiritual mentor and writing in a daily journal.

Working with a sponsor
The practice of choosing a confidant, or what in the Celtic tradition is called a "soul-friend," is an ancient custom found in many cultures and many different religions. In this valuable relationship, both participants profit spiritually. Here we find greater consistency and a greater ability to get to know ourselves in depth.

The person we choose should be dependable, trustworthy, hospitable, compassionate—qualities we naturally associate with a friend, and those we look for in a Fifth Step listener. He or she need not be a professional psychologist or an ordained clergyperson.

Yet these people must be, above all, discerners of the heart, people who understand and accept others as they are learning to have compassion for themselves. This soul-friend, quite simply, should be someone who is attempting to live a spirituality similar to that described in the Twelve Steps.

Using a journal
Through a personal journal or log, we can make an inventory of our lives each day. We can record in it the events and people that have had their effects on us; the areas of life where we feel angry, guilty, alienated, and resentful; the signs of positive growth; the barriers transcended; and the reasons to give thanks.

Even dreams can be recorded for later recall and reflection. These speak to us in the darkness of the night about unknown aspects of ourselves and new, creative possibilities.

Such a log or journal is meant to be not merely a calendar of events or a superficial diary, but a real effort to learn more about ourselves: who we are and where we're going. This journal in all its honesty can be referred to when we're preparing the next Fifth Step. Parts of it can serve even as a basis of the Fifth Step itself.

When we decide it is time to make another Fifth Step, we should recognize that we need not go back over our whole lives, but rather take up where we left off when the last Fifth Step was made. What is past is past. What we acknowledged once need not be discussed again unless certain incidents or feelings have recurred or we finally recognize a pattern of behavior we overlooked.

Developing a spirituality of reconciliation

Every Fifth Step is an opportunity for more self-knowledge and self-acceptance. It can also teach us the importance of forgiveness and reconciliation. This is one of the major lessons that we learn from AA: how necessary it is to develop a spirituality of reconciliation in our daily lives, one that affirms spiritual progress rather than spiritual perfection.

Turning toward a new way of life

The genius of AA's co-founder Bill Wilson is that he understood human nature and the nature of a spiritual awakening that leads to reconciliation. This was clear when he wrote down the Twelve Steps for the first time. Based on his own struggles with power-lessness and his Higher Power, he understood that such an awakening, if it is to continue or even happen to anyone, means more than abstinence. It means more than merely turning away from alcohol or other fatal addictions. It means turning *toward* something or someone else. It means fully embracing a new way of life.

This new spirituality means reaching out, often when we feel least capable of doing so, to a supportive group of friends and to a Higher Power who may at times seem more absent than present. Developing a spirituality of reconciliation is fundamentally about learning to trust our Higher Power and stop trying to play God ourselves.

Focusing on ourselves
This spirituality is also about focusing on ourselves—our own human limitations and forms of sickness that color all our lives—rather than concentrating our attention upon the failures, frailties, and faults of others. Instead, we attempt to recognize our own. We seek to name those broken, raw areas of our lives and personalities that continue to cause us and others frustration and sometimes great pain. And through our daily inventories, we act upon our insights, our guilt and unhappiness, our yearning to change. We open ourselves up to new possibilities; we make ourselves ready, through prayer, for the courage that will bring change about. Daily, in different and often ordinary ways, we go to one another to be forgiven; and when asked for forgiveness, we are ready to give it. Sometimes this happens only with the help of prayer and the healing balm of time.

If we are parents, we try to change ourselves first by recognizing old, sometimes inherited, often unconscious, patterns of behavior. (We might do this with help from a spiritual mentor or soul-friend.) With that painful recognition, we attempt to model for our children new patterns of relating to others and of dealing with stress or just plain tiredness. When conflict has occurred between us, we openly ask forgiveness of our spouses in front of our children. We ask forgiveness of our children for the mistakes we make or the anger expressed inappropriately.

We begin to teach children by our example that to be human is to err, that those who love each other will experience disagreements, and that all of us need to seek forgiveness and to make restitution for wrongs done. Daily inventories during some suitable time of quiet meditation or prayer often reveal what needs to be done to heal wounds and areas of outright neglect—not only in our personal lives, but in our churches, culture, and society.

Taking Step Five at the turning points

Sometimes conflict is especially severe, such as when we discover destructive patterns are more deeply rooted than we had imagined, or when we experience confusion, loss, and the deep awareness that something must change. (And it is probably us!) At those times, Steps Four and Five can help anyone. This is especially true at mid-life and other major life junctures. It is then that we have the most to gain from the healing power of such self-disclosure.

Whether we are at a turning point, in a time of crisis, or when we are simply living with our daily responsibilities, a spirituality of reconciliation can

21

eventually result in new feelings of gratitude, joy, and hope. Such feelings often invite and challenge us to more conscious and committed forms of service advocated by Step Twelve. For, as Bill Wilson once said, "Life gives us moments, and for those moments we give our lives."

Summary

This pamphlet has covered a lot of ground in relation to Step Five. The following are some key points:

Start with Step Four
Make time for the Step Four inventory. Set aside a quiet place for doing it, gather the needed materials, and simply begin writing. To get started, divide your life into ten-year periods. Then look for examples of resentment, fear, and guilt—any of the character defects or secrets tied to your unhappiness. It's important to be honest and thorough. At the same time, avoid perfectionism and strive for balance—be sure to note your assets as well your defects.

Choose a friendly listener
While doing your Fourth Step, look for someone who can listen to your Fifth Step. Find a person who can keep what you say in confidence—someone who understands the Fifth Step. The ideal person will bring wisdom and maturity to the job of listening and will be willing to share some incidents from his or her own life as well.

Tell your story
Sit down with your Fifth Step listener, acknowledge any feelings of fear or guilt, and then simply begin

22

your story. Use the results of your Fourth Step inventory as a guide, not a script. Begin with your childhood and work up to the present, telling all that you need to tell. And remember that the purpose of this Step is to heal yourself—not to please the listener.

Let go and let God
Your Fifth Step will be different from anyone else's. If you have a dramatic or spiritual experience, that's fine. Keep in mind, however, that we do not control the results of this Step. That's up to a Higher Power. What counts is not "results," but whether we are honest and thorough.

Make the Fifth Step an ongoing event
The Fifth Step can be a regular event in our lives. Many choose to "clean house" by taking this Step once or twice a year. As we do, working with a sponsor and writing in a journal can be powerful tools.

Applying these ideas can make reconciliation a whole new way of life. We move from resentment to forgiveness, from perfectionism to spiritual progress, from isolation to reaching out to others, and from powerlessness to trust in a Higher Power.

Conclusion: Finding courage

There is one thing lacking in any guide to the Fifth Step that no theoretical description can provide: the courage to proceed with Step Five. For such courage, we can only make ourselves ready and pray for the power to carry it out—realizing that if we do not take this vital Step, the process of spiritual awakening may not occur.

Whenever we are considering the Fifth Step and feeling hesitant about taking it, we should know that we are not alone. Many before us have felt the same hesitation. We share with them a common story. It is difficult to live as we were meant to live. We learn slowly, step by faltering step, like a child learning to walk. We learn painfully in the school of suffering. One day, however, recognizing our powerlessness, we learn surrender and what it means to pray; what it means, finally, to take the risk so that new life can be born.

The Twelve Steps of Alcoholics Anonymous[*]

1. We admitted we were powerless over alcohol—
   that our lives had become unmanageable.
2. Came to believe that a Power greater than ourselves could restore us to sanity.
3. Made a decision to turn our will and our lives
   over to the care of God *as we understood Him.*
4. Made a searching and fearless moral inventory of
   ourselves.
5. Admitted to God, to ourselves, and to another
   human being the exact nature of our wrongs.
6. Were entirely ready to have God remove all these
   defects of character.
7. Humbly asked Him to remove our shortcomings.
8. Made a list of all persons we had harmed, and
   became willing to make amends to them all.
9. Made direct amends to such people wherever
   possible, except when to do so would injure them
   or others.
10. Continued to take personal inventory and when
    we were wrong promptly admitted it.
11. Sought through prayer and meditation to im-
    prove our conscious contact with God *as we
    understood Him,* praying only for knowledge of
    His will for us and the power to carry that out.
12. Having had a spiritual awakening as the result
    of these steps, we tried to carry this message to
    alcoholics, and to practice these principles in all
    our affairs.

---

[*]The Twelve Steps of AA are taken from *Alcoholics Anonymous,* 3d
ed., published by AA World Services, Inc., New York, N.Y., 59-60.
Reprinted with permission of AA World Services, Inc. (See editor's
note on the copyright page.)

About Hazelden Publishing

As part of the Hazelden Betty Ford Foundation, Hazelden Publishing offers both cutting-edge educational resources and inspirational books. Our print and digital works help guide individuals in treatment and recovery, and their loved ones. Professionals who work to prevent and treat addiction also turn to Hazelden Publishing for evidence-based curricula, digital content solutions, and videos for use in schools, treatment programs, correctional programs, and electronic health records systems. We also offer training for implementation of our curricula.

Through published and digital works, Hazelden Publishing extends the reach of healing and hope to individuals, families, and communities affected by addiction and related issues.

For more information about Hazelden publications, please call **800-328-9000** or visit us online at **hazelden.org/bookstore.**